DO ONE THING EVERY DAY THAT SCARES YOU.

A journal of 365 acts of bravery by

Melissa

"DO ONE THING EVERY DAY THAT SCARES YOU."

THAT CHALLENGE

is attributed to Eleanor Roosevelt, who had good reason to look for ways to overcome fear. She was a shy, frightened little girl, with a gawky appearance and a personal life touched by sadness. Yet, thrust onto the public stage after her marriage to Franklin, Eleanor was able to build courage and daring and emerge as a national and international icon, social activist, role model, and inspiration to people around the world.

How about you? Are you afraid of something physical—diving, skiing, skating, throwing a ball? Or are your fears psychological? Afraid to speak in public? Say "no" to your boss? Or do you have phobias about snakes or mirrors or dentists? Afraid to change your look, ask for a raise, talk to a stranger, bake a cassoulet, go to a rave or opera, return to school?

We all have a different risk tolerance, a wall that defines the borders of our comfort zone. What is yours? Begin by making a list of things that scare you—big and small. Then, after a year of recording daily acts of bravery, make a list of things that no longer scare you. By taking small, regular, and deliberate steps, you will start to notice that the wall has retreated and your comfort zone expanded.

You may want to fill out the 365 pages of this journal one after the other, as in a traditional diary. Or you may prefer to flip through to find the quote that fires your spirit on a particular day. The date lines are blank, awaiting your decision.

So—"Now's the day, and now's the hour," as Robert Burns said. By doing one thing every day that scares you, you may discover that you have changed your world and possibly *the* world, too.

DATE: 8/16/14

A list of things that scare me:

- being alone in a strange place
- spiders
- creepy crawly bugs
- not being able to contact M + D
- airport security

BEHOLD THE TURTLE. HE MAKES PROGRESS ONLY WHEN HE STICKS HIS NECK OUT.

James Bryant Conant

Today I stuck my neck out by:

_____

_____

_____

I am a writer
who came from
a sheltered life.
A sheltered life
can be a daring
life as well. For
all serious daring
starts from within.

Eudora Welty

My inner daring today:

_____

_____

_____

DATE: __/__/__

THE HARDER PATH TODAY:

_____

_____

_____

_____

_____

_____

_____

DATE: __/__/__

THE HARDER PATH TODAY:

_____

_____

_____

_____

_____

_____

_____

When two paths open before you, take the harder one.

Nepalese proverb

EVERY TIME YOU WIN, IT DIMINISHES THE FEAR A LITTLE BIT. YOU NEVER REALLY CANCEL THE FEAR OF LOSING; YOU KEEP CHALLENGING IT.

Arthur Ashe

My fear:

_____

_____

_____

I challenged it today by:

_____

_____

_____

INSIDE OF A RING OR OUT, AIN'T NOTHING WRONG WITH GOING DOWN. IT'S STAYING DOWN THAT'S WRONG.

Muhammad Ali

Today I went down and got back up:

_____

_____

_____

DATE: __/__/__

A hard decision I need to make:

_____

_____

_____

What I decided:

_____

_____

_____

_____

_____

_____

_____

_____

_____

_____

DATE: __/__/__

THE RISK OF A WRONG DECISION IS PREFERABLE TO THE TERROR OF INDECISION.

Maimonides

Today I made this decision in spite of the risk:

_____

_____

_____

What happened?

_____

_____

_____

DATE: __/__/__

TRY A THING YOU HAVEN'T DONE THREE TIMES. ONCE, TO GET OVER THE FEAR OF DOING IT. TWICE, TO LEARN HOW TO DO IT. AND A THIRD TIME TO FIGURE OUT WHETHER YOU LIKE IT OR NOT.

Virgil Thomson

I tried _____ for the first time.

[ ] SECOND TIME __/__/__

[ ] THIRD TIME __/__/__

LIKE IT? [ ] YES [ ] NO

He that observeth
the wind cannot
sow; and he that
regardeth the
clouds shall
not reap.

Ecclesiastes 11:4

Today I:

_____

_____

_____

DATE: __/__/__

AT ___ O'CLOCK

Today I:

_____

_____

_____

_____

_____

_____

_____

DATE: __/__/__

AT ___ O'CLOCK

Today I:

_____

_____

_____

_____

_____

_____

_____

NOW'S THE DAY, AND NOW'S THE HOUR.

Robert Burns

| GO OUTSIDE YOUR STYLE COMFORT ZONE | Think about possible styles to try and diagram how far they fall outside of your comfort zone. |

terrifying!

reluctant to try

willing to try

my comfort zone

Oh, how I regret not having worn a bikini for the entire year I was twenty-six. If anyone young is reading this, go, right this minute, put on a bikini, and don't take it off until you're thirty-four.

Nora Ephron

Today I ventured outside my style comfort zone by wearing:

_____

_____

_____

DATE: __/__/__

MY FAVORITE THING IS TO GO WHERE I'VE NEVER BEEN.

Diane Arbus

Today I went somewhere new:

_____

_____

_____

FOR MY PART, I TRAVEL NOT TO GO ANYWHERE, BUT TO GO. I TRAVEL FOR TRAVEL'S SAKE. THE GREAT AFFAIR IS TO MOVE.

Robert Louis Stevenson

Where I moved today:

_____

_____

_____

"YES!"

Today I said "Yes!" to:

_____

_____

_____

_____

_____

_____

_____

_____

"NO!"

Today I said "No!" to:

_____

_____

_____

_____

_____

_____

_____

_____

DATE: _/_/_

TODAY I RESISTED THIS FEAR:

_____

_____

_____

_____

_____

_____

_____

DATE: _/_/_

TODAY I MASTERED THIS FEAR:

_____

_____

_____

_____

_____

_____

_____

COURAGE IS RESISTANCE TO FEAR, MASTERY OF FEAR, NOT ABSENCE OF FEAR.

Mark Twain

DATE: _/_/_

Just dash something down if you see a blank canvas staring at you with a certain imbecility. You do not know how paralyzing it is, that staring of a blank canvas which says to the painter, You don't know anything.

Vincent van Gogh

Today I dashed down:

_____

_____

_____

DATE: __/__/__

Dare to create art today. Draw, scribble,
or doodle something right here, right now:

I AM NOT AFRAID OF STORMS, FOR I AM LEARNING HOW TO SAIL MY SHIP.

Louisa May Alcott

Storms I sailed through today:

_____

_____

_____

DATE: __/__/__

I LOVE TO SAIL FORBIDDEN SEAS, AND LAND ON BARBAROUS COASTS.

Herman Melville

Today's forbidden seas:

_____

_____

_____

One cannot refuse to eat just because there is a chance of choking.

Chinese proverb

Today I tried a new:

[ ] **FOOD**

[ ] **MARKET**

[ ] **RESTAURANT**

[ ] **RECIPE**

[ ] **SEASONING**

[ ] **SOMETHING SCARIER:**

_____

_____

_____

WE KIDS FEARED
MANY THINGS IN THOSE DAYS—
WEREWOLVES, DENTISTS, NORTH
KOREANS, SUNDAY SCHOOL—
BUT THEY ALL PALED IN
COMPARISON WITH
BRUSSELS SPROUTS.

Dave Barry

Today I ate:

_____

_____

_____

DATE: ___/___/___

HOW I WAS BOLD TODAY:

_____

_____

_____

_____

_____

_____

_____

DATE: ___/___/___

HOW I WAS BOLD TODAY:

_____

_____

_____

_____

_____

_____

_____

BE BOLD,
BE BOLD,
AND
EVERY-
WHERE
BE BOLD.

Edmund Spenser

DATE: __/__/__

Rate your social anxiety in the following situations from 1 to 10:

____ MEETING SOMEONE NEW

____ SPEAKING TO A STRANGER ON THE PHONE

____ GOING ON A BLIND DATE

____ GOING TO A PARTY

____ GOING TO A PARTY ALONE

____ PAYING A COMPLIMENT

____ ACCEPTING A COMPLIMENT

____ DEFENDING YOURSELF

____ STATING A CONTRARY OPINION

____ CORRECTING SOMEONE

____ ASKING FOR HELP

____ SOMETHING SCARIER:

_____

_____

_____

IF THERE ARE TWO HUNDRED PEOPLE IN A ROOM AND ONE OF THEM DOESN'T LIKE ME, I'VE GOT TO GET OUT.

Marlon Brando

My social courage today:

_____

_____

_____

YOU'LL ALWAYS MISS 100% OF THE SHOTS YOU DON'T TAKE.

Wayne Gretzky

Today I took this shot:

_____

_____

_____

DATE: __/__/__

ANYONE WHO HAS NEVER MADE A MISTAKE HAS NEVER TRIED ANYTHING NEW.

Albert Einstein

Oops! Today I:

_____

_____

_____

DATE: __/__/__

A NEW FOOD: _____

Rating: [ ] FEH!   [ ] MEH ...   [ ] YEH!

_____

_____

_____

_____

_____

_____

DATE: __/__/__

A NEW RESTAURANT: _____

Review:

_____

_____

_____

_____

_____

_____

HE WAS A BOLD MAN THAT FIRST ATE AN OYSTER.

Jonathan Swift

There is no experience from which you can't learn something. . . . [T]he purpose of life, after all, is to live it, to taste experience to the utmost, to reach out eagerly and without fear for newer and richer experience.

Eleanor Roosevelt

Today's experience:

_____

_____

_____

What I learned:

_____

_____

_____

Experience gives us the tests first and the lessons later.

Naomi Judd

Today's test:

_____

_____

_____

Today's lesson:

_____

_____

_____

START BY DOING WHAT'S NECESSARY; THEN DO WHAT'S POSSIBLE; AND SUDDENLY YOU ARE DOING THE IMPOSSIBLE.

▲
St. Francis of Assisi
▼

Today I:

_____

_____

_____

_____ (Impossible!)

DATE: __/__/__

MOST OF THE THINGS WORTH DOING IN THE WORLD HAD BEEN DECLARED IMPOSSIBLE BEFORE THEY WERE DONE.

Louis D. Brandeis

Today I did something worth doing:

_____

_____

_____

_____ (Impossible!)

DATE: __/__/__

ONE DOES NOT DISCOVER NEW LANDS WITHOUT CONSENTING TO LOSE SIGHT OF THE SHORE FOR A VERY LONG TIME.

André Gide

Today I traveled to:

[ ] A NEW NEIGHBORHOOD

[ ] A NEW STREET

[ ] A NEW PARK

[ ] A NEW LAND

[ ] SOMEPLACE SCARIER:

_____

_____

_____

A SHIP IN PORT IS SAFE, BUT THAT IS NOT WHAT SHIPS ARE BUILT FOR.

Rear Admiral Grace Murray Hopper

Today I:

_____

_____

_____

DATE: __/__/__

MY BRAVE ACT:

_____

_____

_____

MY GOOD FORTUNE:

_____

_____

_____

DATE: __/__/__

ANOTHER BRAVE ACT:

_____

_____

_____

ANOTHER GOOD FORTUNE:

_____

_____

_____

FORTUNE FAVORS THE BRAVE.

Terence

DATE: __/__/__

"YES!"

Today I said "Yes!" to a new project:

_____

_____

_____

_____

_____

_____

_____

_____

"NO!"

Today I said "No!" to a new project:

_____

_____

_____

_____

_____

_____

_____

_____

I HAVE A PHOBIA:
I DON'T LIKE MIRRORS.
AND I DON'T WATCH
MYSELF ON TELEVISION.
IF ANYTHING COMES ON,
I MAKE THEM SHUT IT
OFF, OR I LEAVE THE ROOM.

Pamela Anderson

What I avoid:

_____

_____

_____

EISOPTROPHOBIA—
THE FEAR OF MIRRORS OR
SEEING ONESELF IN A MIRROR

What I fear seeing in the mirror:

[ ] WRINKLES

[ ] FRECKLES

[ ] PIMPLES

[ ] BAD HAIR

[ ] NO CHIN

[ ] TOO MANY CHINS

[ ] BAD NOSE

[ ] ELEPHANT EARS

[ ] YELLOW TEETH

[ ] NOTHING

[ ] SOMETHING WORSE:

_____

_____

_____

Courage is the most important of all virtues, because without courage you can't practice any other virtue consistently.

Maya Angelou

My courage today:

_____

_____

_____

_____

DATE: __/__/__

COURAGE IS THE LADDER ON WHICH ALL OTHER VIRTUES MOUNT.

Clare Boothe Luce

My courage today:

_____

_____

_____

_____

DATE: ___/___/___

TODAY I DARED TO FAIL:

_____

_____

_____

TODAY I ACHIEVED:

_____

_____

_____

DATE: ___/___/___

TODAY I DARED TO FAIL:

_____

_____

_____

TODAY I ACHIEVED:

_____

_____

_____

ONLY THOSE WHO DARE TO FAIL GREATLY CAN EVER ACHIEVE GREATLY.

Robert F. Kennedy

Dare to say "Hi" to a stranger.

Today I said "Hi" to this stranger:

_____

He/she said:

_____

_____

_____

DATE: _/_/_

The more I traveled the more I realized that fear makes strangers of people who should be friends.

Shirley MacLaine

Today I dared to talk to a stranger:

_____

_____

_____

HATE IS THE CONSEQUENCE OF FEAR; WE FEAR SOMETHING BEFORE WE HATE IT; A CHILD WHO FEARS NOISES BECOMES A MAN WHO HATES NOISE.

Cyril Connolly

My fear as a child:

_____

_____

_____

My hate as an adult:

_____

_____

_____

DATE: _/_/_

UNLEARNING IS MORE DIFFICULT THAN LEARNING.

English proverb

A fear I have unlearned:

_____

_____

_____

DATE: __/__/__

> GO OUTSIDE
> YOUR CULTURAL
> COMFORT ZONE

Today I ventured outside my cultural comfort zone by going to:

[ ] AN OPERA

[ ] A BALLET

[ ] A MODERN DANCE

[ ] A DRAMA

[ ] A POETRY SLAM

[ ] A COMEDY CLUB

[ ] AN ART MUSEUM

[ ] AN ART GALLERY

[ ] AN ORCHESTRA PERFORMANCE

[ ] A JAZZ CONCERT

[ ] A RAP CONCERT

[ ] A RAVE

[ ] SOMETHING EVEN SCARIER:

_____

TO BE AN ARTIST MEANS NEVER TO AVERT ONE'S EYES.

Akira Kurosawa

Today I saw:

_____

_____

_____

DATE: __/__/__

TODAY'S DARING ADVENTURE:

_____

_____

_____

_____

_____

_____

_____

DATE: __/__/__

TODAY'S DARING ADVENTURE:

_____

_____

_____

_____

_____

_____

_____

LIFE IS EITHER A DARING ADVENTURE OR NOTHING.

Helen Keller

THE MILL GAINS BY GOING, AND NOT BY STANDING STILL.

Portuguese proverb

Today I:

_____

_____

_____

Life happened because I turned the pages.

Alberto Manguel

Today I dared to turn this page:

_____

_____

_____

You have the gift of life. You've got to get out there and eat it.

Meryl Streep

How I ate life today:

_____

_____

_____

RISK! RISK ANYTHING!...
DO THE HARDEST THING
ON EARTH FOR YOU.
ACT FOR YOURSELF.
FACE THE TRUTH.

Katherine Mansfield

Today I did the hardest thing on earth for me:

_____

_____

_____

IT WAS ONLY AFTER THE FIRST HEBREW JUMPED INTO THE WATER THAT THE RED SEA PARTED.

Anonymous

Scary jump today:

_____

_____

_____

DATE: __/__/__

LIVING AT RISK IS JUMPING OFF THE CLIFF AND BUILDING YOUR WINGS ON THE WAY DOWN.

Ray Bradbury

Scary jump today:

_____

_____

_____

DATE: __/__/__

I WAS A CHAMPION TODAY:

_____

_____

_____

_____

_____

_____

_____

DATE: __/__/__

I WAS A CHAMPION TODAY:

_____

_____

_____

_____

_____

_____

_____

A
champion
is one who
gets up
when he
can't.

Jack Dempsey

DATE: __/__/__

REMEMBERING THAT YOU ARE GOING TO DIE IS THE BEST WAY I KNOW TO AVOID THE TRAP OF THINKING YOU HAVE SOMETHING TO LOSE.

Steve Jobs

Today I:

_____

_____

_____ **What do I have to lose?**

IF MY DOCTOR TOLD ME I HAD ONLY SIX MINUTES TO LIVE, I WOULDN'T BROOD. I'D TYPE A LITTLE FASTER.

Isaac Asimov

If I had only six minutes to live, I would:

_____

_____

_____

DATE: __/__/__

THERE IS NO FAILURE EXCEPT IN NO LONGER TRYING.

Elbert Hubbard

What I tried today:

_____

_____

_____

TO THOSE WHO NEED ENCOURAGEMENT, REMEMBER THIS: BEWARE OF QUITTING TOO SOON. DR. SEUSS'S FIRST CHILDREN'S BOOK WAS REJECTED BY TWENTY-THREE PUBLISHERS. THE TWENTY-FOURTH PUBLISHER SOLD SIX MILLION COPIES.

Ann Landers

How I persisted:

_____

_____

_____

DATE: __/__/__

"YES!"

Today I said "Yes!" when help was offered:

_____
_____
_____
_____
_____
_____
_____
_____
_____

DATE: __/__/__

"NO!"

Today I said "No!" when help was offered:

_____

_____

_____

_____

_____

_____

_____

_____

DATE: _/_/_

FEAR SURMOUNTED:

_____

_____

_____

_____

_____

_____

_____

DATE: _/_/_

FEAR SURMOUNTED:

_____

_____

_____

_____

_____

_____

_____

HE HAS NOT LEARNED THE LESSON OF LIFE WHO DOES NOT EVERY DAY SURMOUNT A FEAR.

Ralph Waldo Emerson

DATE: __/__/__

I DON'T LIKE TO GO INTO ELEVATORS. I DON'T GO THROUGH TUNNELS. I LIKE THE DRAIN IN THE SHOWER TO BE IN THE CORNER AND NOT IN THE MIDDLE.

Woody Allen

Do you share Woody's fears?

ELEVATORS? [ ] YES [ ] NO

TUNNELS? [ ] YES [ ] NO

SHOWER DRAINS? [ ] YES [ ] NO

THE MORE WARY YOU ARE OF DANGER, THE MORE LIKELY YOU ARE TO MEET IT.

Jean de La Fontaine

Today I:

_____

_____

_____

THE PRICE OF DOING THE SAME OLD THING IS FAR HIGHER THAN THE PRICE OF CHANGE.

Bill Clinton

The same old thing:

_____

_____

_____

How I changed it today:

_____

_____

_____

DATE: __/__/__

BETWEEN TWO EVILS, I LIKE TO PICK THE ONE I HAVEN'T TRIED BEFORE.

Mae West

Evil 1:

_____

Evil 2:

_____

My choice:

_____

DATE: __/__/__

GO OUTSIDE
YOUR HAIRSTYLE
COMFORT ZONE

Think about possible hairstyles to
try and diagram how far they fall
outside of your comfort zone.

terrifying!

reluctant to try

willing to try

my comfort zone

DATE: __/__/__

In Hollywood a girl's virtue is much less important than her hairdo.

Marilyn Monroe

Today I ventured outside my comfort zone by changing my hairstyle:

_____

_____

_____

DATE: __/__/__

WHAT I BEGAN TODAY:

_____

_____

_____

_____

_____

_____

_____

DATE: __/__/__

WHAT I BEGAN TODAY:

_____

_____

_____

_____

_____

_____

_____

ALL GLORY COMES FROM DARING TO BEGIN.

Anonymous

Dare to be creative with words today:
Write the first line of a

[ ] POEM

[ ] NOVEL

[ ] ESSAY

[ ] LETTER

[ ] MEMOIR

[ ] OTHER: _____

My first line:

_____

_____

_____

_____

_____

_____

_____

DATE: __/__/__

I DIP MY PEN IN THE BLACKEST INK, BECAUSE I'M NOT AFRAID OF FALLING INTO MY INKPOT.

Ralph Waldo Emerson

Today I:

_____

_____

_____

DATE: __/__/__

EVEN IF YOU'RE ON THE RIGHT TRACK, YOU'LL GET RUN OVER IF YOU JUST SIT THERE.

Will Rogers

The direction I *moved* on the right track:

_____

_____

_____

Curiosity will conquer fear even more than bravery will.

James Stephens

My curiosity today:

_____

_____

_____

DATE: __/__/__

TODAY I SHOWED COURAGE BY:

_____

_____

_____

_____

_____

_____

_____

DATE: __/__/__

TODAY I SHOWED COURAGE BY:

_____

_____

_____

_____

_____

_____

_____

THE TRUE COURAGE IS FACING DANGER WHEN YOU ARE AFRAID.

L. Frank Baum

DATE: __/__/__

Rate your hypochondria.

Where does it hurt?
Mark your ailments
and rate their severity
from 1 to 10.

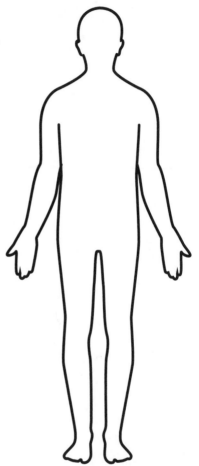

DATE: __/__/__

I TOLD THE DOCTOR I WAS OVERTIRED, ANXIETY-RIDDEN, COMPULSIVELY ACTIVE, CONSTANTLY DEPRESSED, WITH RECURRING FITS OF PARANOIA. TURNS OUT I'M NORMAL.

Jules Feiffer

Today I:

_____

_____

_____

Two roads diverged
in a wood, and I—

I took the one less
traveled by,

And that has made
all the difference.

Robert Frost

Road not taken:

_____

_____

_____

Road taken:

_____

_____

_____

WHEN YOU COME TO A FORK IN THE ROAD, TAKE IT.

Yogi Berra

Today I:

_____

_____

_____

AH, BUT A MAN'S REACH SHOULD EXCEED HIS GRASP,

OR WHAT'S A HEAVEN FOR?

Robert Browning

Today I reached for:

_____

_____

_____

THE RIPEST PEACH IS HIGHEST ON THE TREE.

James Whitcomb Riley

My peach:

_____

_____

_____

DATE: __/__/__

TODAY I STARTED TO CHANGE MY LIFE:

_____

_____

_____

_____

_____

_____

_____

DATE: __/__/__

TODAY I STARTED TO CHANGE MY LIFE:

_____

_____

_____

_____

_____

_____

_____

TO CHANGE ONE'S LIFE: START IMMEDIATELY. DO IT FLAMBOYANTLY. NO EXCEPTIONS.

William James

GROWTH DEMANDS A TEMPORARY SURRENDER OF SECURITY.

Gail Sheehy

Security I surrendered today:

_____

_____

_____

LIFE SHRINKS OR EXPANDS IN PROPORTION TO ONE'S COURAGE.

Anaïs Nin

How my life has expanded:

_____

_____

_____

_____

DON'T BE AFRAID TO TAKE A BIG STEP IF ONE IS INDICATED. YOU CAN'T CROSS A CHASM IN TWO SMALL JUMPS.

David Lloyd George

My small jump:

_____

My small jump:

_____

My BIG STEP:

_____

HE THAT STAYS IN THE VALLEY SHALL NEVER GET OVER THE HILL.

English proverb

Today I:

_____

_____

_____

DATE: __/__/__

I SEIZED TODAY:

_____

_____

_____

_____

_____

_____

_____

DATE: __/__/__

I SEIZED TODAY:

_____

_____

_____

_____

_____

_____

_____

SEIZE THE DAY; PUT NO TRUST IN TOMORROW.

Horace

"YES!"

Today I said "Yes!" to an outrageous idea:

_____

_____

_____

_____

_____

_____

_____

"NO!"

Today I said "No!" to an outrageous idea:

_____

_____

_____

_____

_____

_____

_____

_____

I THINK I CAN,
I THINK I CAN,
I THINK I CAN.

Watty Piper

I think I can:

_____

I think I can:

_____

I think I can:

_____

THINK YOU CAN, THINK YOU CAN'T; EITHER WAY, YOU'LL BE RIGHT.

Henry Ford

Today I thought I could:

_____

_____

_____

What happened?

_____

_____

_____

DATE: _/_/_

I have three phobias which, could I mute them, would make my life as slick as a sonnet, but as dull as ditch water: I hate to go to bed, I hate to get up, and I hate to be alone.

Tallulah Bankhead

A phobia that makes my life exciting:

_____

_____

_____

FEAR ITSELF MADE HER DARING.

Ovid

Today I:

_____

_____

_____

DATE: __/__/__

TODAY'S DEED:

_____

_____

_____

TODAY'S RISK:

_____

_____

_____

DATE: __/__/__

TODAY'S DEED:

_____

_____

_____

TODAY'S RISK:

_____

_____

_____

GREAT DEEDS ARE USUALLY WROUGHT AT GREAT RISKS.

Herodotus

OF ALL FORMS OF CAUTION, CAUTION IN LOVE IS PERHAPS THE MOST FATAL TO TRUE HAPPINESS.

Bertrand Russell

Today I was incautious:

_____

_____

_____

Being deeply loved by someone gives you strength, while loving someone deeply gives you courage.

Lao Tzu

My love today:

_____

_____

_____

DATE: __/__/__

| GO OUTSIDE YOUR ATHLETIC COMFORT ZONE | Think about possible sports to try and diagram how far they fall outside of your comfort zone. |

terrifying!

reluctant to try

willing to try

my comfort zone

COURAGE IS BEING SCARED TO DEATH… AND SADDLING UP ANYWAY.

John Wayne

Today I ventured outside my athletic comfort zone by:

_____

_____

_____

DATE: __/__/__

TODAY'S GAINS:

_____

_____

_____

TODAY'S PAINS:

_____

_____

_____

DATE: __/__/__

TODAY'S GAINS:

_____

_____

_____

TODAY'S PAINS:

_____

_____

_____

THERE ARE NO GAINS WITHOUT PAINS.

Benjamin Franklin

DATE: __/__/__

Dare to change the world today (choose one):

[ ] **IN YOUR NEIGHBORHOOD**

[ ] **IN YOUR CITY**

[ ] **IN YOUR STATE**

[ ] **IN YOUR COUNTRY**

[ ] **IN THE WORLD**

[ ] **ON THE PLANET**

Today I:

_____

_____

_____

_____

_____

_____

_____

Die when I may, I want
it said of me by those
who know me best, that
I have always plucked
a thistle and planted a
flower where I thought
a flower would grow.

Abraham Lincoln

Today I:

_____

_____

_____

WE HAVE TOO MANY HIGH-SOUNDING WORDS AND TOO FEW ACTIONS THAT CORRESPOND WITH THEM.

Abigail Adams

My words today:

_____

_____

_____

My actions today:

_____

_____

_____

DATE: __/__/__

SPEAK
LITTLE.
DO MUCH.

Benjamin Franklin

My words:

_____

_____

_____

My actions:

_____

_____

_____

GO WEST, YOUNG MAN.

Horace Greeley

My next adventure will be:

_____

_____

_____

THE FRONTIERS ARE NOT EAST OR WEST, NORTH OR SOUTH, BUT WHEREVER A MAN FRONTS A FACT.

Henry David Thoreau

Fact I dared to confront today:

_____

_____

_____

DATE: __/__/__

TODAY I WAS BRAVE:

_____

_____

_____

_____

_____

_____

_____

DATE: __/__/__

TODAY I WAS BRAVE:

_____

_____

_____

_____

_____

_____

_____

NONE BUT THE BRAVE DESERVES THE FAIR.

John Dryden

PEOPLE WISH TO LEARN TO SWIM AND AT THE SAME TIME TO KEEP ONE FOOT ON THE GROUND.

Marcel Proust

Today I took my foot off the ground:

_____

_____

_____

To act is to be committed, and to be committed is to be in danger.

James Baldwin

Today I made this commitment:

_____

_____

_____

DATE: __/__/__

IF THOU FOLLOW THY STAR, THOU CANST NOT FAIL OF A GLORIOUS HEAVEN.

Dante

My star:

_____

_____

_____

HE TURNS NOT BACK WHO IS BOUND TO A STAR.

Leonardo da Vinci

Today I:

_____

_____

_____

DATE: __/__/__

TODAY I SHARED MY COURAGE BY:

_____

_____

_____

_____

_____

_____

_____

DATE: __/__/__

TODAY I SHARED MY COURAGE BY:

_____

_____

_____

_____

_____

_____

_____

Keep your fears to yourself but share your courage.

Robert Louis Stevenson

YOU CANNOT FIND WHAT YOU DO NOT SEEK. YOU CANNOT GRASP WHEN YOU DO NOT REACH. YOUR DREAMS WON'T COME UP TO YOUR FRONT DOOR. YOU HAVE GOT TO TAKE A LEAP, IF YOU WANT TO SOAR.

Cory Booker

Today I took this leap:

_____

_____

_____

The artist never entirely knows. We guess. We may be wrong, but we take leap after leap in the dark.

Agnes de Mille

Today I took this leap:

_____

_____

_____

DATE: __/__/__

"YES!"

Today I said "Yes!" to a friend:

_____

_____

_____

_____

_____

_____

_____

_____

"NO!"

Today I said "No!" to a friend:

_____

_____

_____

_____

_____

_____

_____

_____

THE ONLY THING WE HAVE TO FEAR IS FEAR ITSELF.

Franklin Delano Roosevelt

Today I:

_____

_____

_____

DATE: __/__/__

FEAR MAKES THE WOLF BIGGER THAN IT IS.

German proverb

Today I shrunk this "wolf":

_____

_____

_____

DATE: __/__/__

GOAL:

_____

_____

_____

STEP 1:

_____

_____

_____

DATE: __/__/__

GOAL:

_____

_____

_____

STEP 1:

_____

_____

_____

THE FIRST STEP IS THE HARDEST.

English proverb

I LIKE THE DREAMS OF THE FUTURE BETTER THAN THE HISTORY OF THE PAST.

Thomas Jefferson

My dream of the future:

_____

_____

_____

DATE: __/__/__

YOU'RE NEVER TOO OLD TO SET ANOTHER GOAL OR TO DREAM A NEW DREAM.

C. S. Lewis

My new dream:

_____

_____

_____

I'll take heart
And make a start—

Though I fear the
prospect's shady—

Much I'd spend
To gain my end—

Faint heart never
won fair lady!

W. S. Gilbert

Start I made today:

_____

_____

_____

DATE: __/__/__

THE LOVING ARE THE DARING.

Bayard Taylor

Whom I love:

_____

_____

_____

What I dared:

_____

_____

_____

DATE: __/__/__

Dare to change your look today (choose one).

    [ ] HAIR

    [ ] FACE

    [ ] CLOTHES

    [ ] SHOES

    [ ] COLOR

    [ ] STYLE

Today I:

_____

_____

_____

_____

_____

_____

_____

WHY DON'T YOU TURN YOUR OLD ERMINE COAT INTO A BATHROBE?

▲
Diana Vreeland
▼

Today I:

_____

_____

_____

DATE: __/__/__

TODAY'S GRAIN OF BOLDNESS:

_____

_____

_____

_____

_____

_____

_____

DATE: __/__/__

TODAY'S GRAIN OF BOLDNESS:

_____

_____

_____

_____

_____

_____

_____

PUT A GRAIN OF BOLDNESS INTO EVERYTHING YOU DO.

Baltasar Gracián

| GO OUTSIDE YOUR TRAVEL COMFORT ZONE | Think about possible places to go and diagram how far they fall outside of your comfort zone. |

terrifying!

reluctant to try

willing to try

my comfort zone

I live my life in widening circles that reach out across the world.

Rainer Maria Rilke

Today I ventured outside my travel comfort zone by planning a trip to:

_____

_____

_____

DATE: ___/___/___

DENTOPHOBIA—
THE FEAR OF DENTISTS

Rate your fear of procedures. *(Assign each a rank from 1 to 10.)*

_____ **CLEANING**

_____ **DRILLING**

_____ **FILLING**

_____ **NOVOCAINE**

_____ **ROOT CANAL**

_____ **X-RAYS**

_____ **PERIODONTIA**

_____ **SOMETHING WORSE:**

_____

_____

_____

_____

_____

_____

_____

AS FOR CONSULTING A
DENTIST REGULARLY, MY
PUNCTUALITY PRACTICALLY
AMOUNTED TO A FETISH.
EVERY TWELVE YEARS I WOULD
DROP WHATEVER I WAS DOING
AND ALLOW WILD CAUCASIAN
PONIES TO DRAG ME TO A
REPUTABLE ORTHODONTIST.

S. J. Perelman

Today I:

_____

_____

_____

DATE: _/_/_

ALL THINGS ARE POSSIBLE UNTIL THEY ARE PROVED IMPOSSIBLE— AND EVEN THE IMPOSSIBLE MAY ONLY BE SO, AS OF NOW.

Pearl S. Buck

I did the "impossible" today:

_____

_____

_____

Somebody said that it couldn't be done,

But he with a chuckle replied

That "maybe it couldn't,"
but he would be one

Who wouldn't say so till he'd tried.

So he buckled right in with
the trace of a grin

On his face. If he worried he hid it.

He started to sing as he
tackled the thing

That couldn't be done, and he did it.

Edgar Guest

Today I did what "couldn't be done":

_____

_____

_____

DATE: __/__/__

I WAS A LION TODAY BY:

_____

_____

_____

_____

_____

_____

_____

DATE: __/__/__

I WAS A LION TODAY BY:

_____

_____

_____

_____

_____

_____

_____

IT IS BETTER TO BE A LION FOR A DAY THAN A SHEEP ALL YOUR LIFE.

Sister Elizabeth Kenny

DATE: __/__/__

Rate your school anxiety from 1 to 10 (even if you are not in school).

_____ ATTENDING THE FIRST DAY OF CLASS

_____ ARRIVING ON TIME

_____ PERFORMING IN FRONT OF CLASSMATES

_____ PREPARING ENOUGH

_____ BEING CALLED ON

_____ TAKING POP QUIZZES

_____ TAKING FINAL EXAMS

_____ RECEIVING YOUR GRADES

_____ SOMETHING SCARIER:

_____

_____

_____

_____

_____

_____

Education is the only interest worthy the deep, controlling anxiety of the thoughtful man.

Wendell Phillips

Today I learned:

_____

_____

_____

WE MUST WALK CONSCIOUSLY ONLY PART WAY TOWARD OUR GOAL, AND THEN LEAP IN THE DARK TO OUR SUCCESS.

Henry David Thoreau

My leap forward today:

_____

_____

_____

THERE ARE SOME THINGS ONE CAN ONLY ACHIEVE BY A DELIBERATE LEAP IN THE OPPOSITE DIRECTION.

Franz Kafka

My leap backward today:

_____

_____

_____

DATE: __/__/__

MY VOYAGE TODAY:

_____

_____

_____

_____

_____

_____

_____

DATE: __/__/__

MY VOYAGE TODAY:

_____

_____

_____

_____

_____

_____

_____

MAKE VOYAGES! ATTEMPT THEM! THERE'S NOTHING ELSE.

Tennessee Williams

You can't catch trout with dry breeches.

Spanish proverb

My "trout":

_____

_____

_____

My "wet breeches":

_____

_____

_____

IT IS EASY TO BE BRAVE FROM A SAFE DISTANCE.

Aesop

Today I came closer to:

_____

_____

_____

DATE: __/__/__

"YES!"

Today at work I said "Yes!" to:

_____

_____

_____

_____

_____

_____

_____

_____

DATE: __/__/__

"NO!"

Today at work I said "No!" to:

_____

_____

_____

_____

_____

_____

_____

_____

_____

DATE: __/__/__

TODAY I THINK I CAN:

_____

_____

_____

_____

_____

_____

_____

DATE: __/__/__

TODAY I THINK I CAN:

_____

_____

_____

_____

_____

_____

_____

THEY CAN BECAUSE THEY THINK THEY CAN.

Virgil

YOU DON'T LEARN TO HOLD YOUR OWN IN THE WORLD BY STANDING ON GUARD, BUT BY ATTACKING, AND GETTING WELL HAMMERED YOURSELF.

George Bernard Shaw

Today I attacked:

_____

_____

_____

How I got hammered:

_____

_____

_____

WHEN YOU WIN, NOTHING HURTS.

Joe Namath

Today I:

_____

_____

_____

Mama exhorted her children at every opportunity to "jump at the sun." We might not land on the sun, but at least we would get off the ground.

Zora Neale Hurston

Today I "jumped at the sun":

_____

_____

_____

DATE: __/__/__

FAR AWAY IN THE SUNSHINE ARE MY HIGHEST INSPIRATIONS. I MAY NOT REACH THEM, BUT I CAN LOOK UP AND SEE THE BEAUTY, BELIEVE IN THEM, AND TRY TO FOLLOW WHERE THEY LEAD.

Louisa May Alcott

My inspiration today:

_____

_____

_____

BOLDNESS, AND AGAIN BOLDNESS, AND ALWAYS BOLDNESS.

Georges Jacques Danton

Today's boldness:

_____

_____

_____

THE CHIEF DANGER IN LIFE IS THAT YOU MAY TAKE TOO MANY PRECAUTIONS.

Alfred Adler

I abandoned these precautions today:

_____

_____

_____

DATE: __/__/__

TODAY'S FEAR WAS ____°.

_____

_____

_____

_____

_____

_____

_____

DATE: __/__/__

TODAY'S FEAR WAS ____°.

_____

_____

_____

_____

_____

_____

_____

THERE IS NO SUCH THING AS BRAVERY, ONLY DEGREES OF FEAR.

John Wainwright

To win without risk is to triumph without glory.

Pierre Corneille

Today's risk:

_____

_____

_____

Today's triumph:

_____

_____

_____

BELIEVE ME! THE SECRET OF REAPING THE GREATEST FRUIT-FULNESS AND THE GREATEST ENJOYMENT FROM LIFE IS TO LIVE DANGEROUSLY!

Friedrich Wilhelm Nietzsche

Today I lived dangerously:

_____

_____

_____

DATE: __/__/__

Dare to think like an entrepreneur today.

These are businesses I could start:

_____

_____

_____

_____

_____

_____

_____

_____

_____

_____

MY INTEREST IN LIFE COMES FROM SETTING MYSELF HUGE, APPARENTLY UNACHIEVABLE CHALLENGES, AND TRYING TO RISE ABOVE THEM.

Richard Branson

Today's huge, apparently unachievable challenge:

_____

_____

_____

DATE: __/__/__

TODAY I DID NOT CAPITULATE:

_____

_____

_____

_____

_____

_____

_____

DATE: __/__/__

TODAY I DID NOT CAPITULATE:

_____

_____

_____

_____

_____

_____

_____

I WILL BE CONQUERED; I WILL NOT CAPITULATE.

Samuel Johnson

DATE: __/__/__

GO OUTSIDE
YOUR NATURAL
COMFORT ZONE

Think about possible ways to interact with
nature and/or animals and diagram how far
they fall outside of your comfort zone.

terrifying!

reluctant to try

willing to try

my comfort zone

I'm not about
to go out and buy
a snake for a pet.
I mean, I may have
faced a few fears
but I'm not insane.

Kristin Davis

Today I ventured outside my natural comfort zone by:

_____

_____

_____

IF YOU WOULD HIT THE MARK, YOU MUST AIM A LITTLE ABOVE IT; EVERY ARROW THAT FLIES FEELS THE ATTRACTION OF THE EARTH.

Henry Wadsworth Longfellow

Today I aimed high:

_____

_____

_____

Four things come not back:

the spoken word; the sped arrow;

time past; and the neglected opportunity.

Omar Ibn Al-Halif

An opportunity I did not neglect today:

_____

_____

_____

DATE: __/__/__

Today I:

_____

_____

_____

_____

_____

_____

_____

DATE: __/__/__

Today I:

_____

_____

_____

_____

_____

_____

_____

NOTHING IS HARDER ON YOUR LAURELS THAN RESTING ON THEM.

Anonymous

DATE: __/__/__

AVIOPHOBIA—
THE FEAR OF
FLYING

My aviophobias:

[ ] HELIUM BALLOON

[ ] SPACESHIP

[ ] HELICOPTER

[ ] GLIDER

[ ] SUPERSONIC TRANSPORT

[ ] BIPLANE

[ ] NONE

[ ] SOMETHING SCARIER:

_____

_____

_____

_____

DATE: __/__/__

Years ago, I discovered that I could keep the plane I was flying on from crashing by refusing to adjust my watch to the new time zone until we were on the ground, and I have used that method ever since.

Calvin Trillin

My secret method for overcoming a phobia:

_____

_____

_____

COWARDS DIE MANY TIMES BEFORE THEIR DEATHS:

THE VALIANT NEVER TASTE OF DEATH BUT ONCE.

William Shakespeare

Today I was not a coward:

_____

_____

_____

DATE: __/__/__

IT IS BETTER TO DIE ON YOUR FEET THAN TO LIVE ON YOUR KNEES.

Emiliano Zapata

Today I stood tall:

_____

_____

_____

LIFE IS LIKE A TEN-SPEED BIKE. MOST OF US HAVE GEARS WE NEVER USE.

Charles Schulz

What I could do if I used all of my gears:

_____

_____

_____

DATE: _/_/_

LIFE IS LIKE RIDING A BICYCLE.
TO KEEP YOUR BALANCE, YOU MUST KEEP MOVING.

Albert Einstein

Where I moved today:

_____

_____

_____

DATE: __/__/__

HOW I GREW TODAY:

_____

_____

_____

_____

_____

_____

_____

DATE: __/__/__

HOW I GREW TODAY:

_____

_____

_____

_____

_____

_____

_____

BE NOT AFRAID OF GROWING SLOWLY, BE AFRAID ONLY OF STANDING STILL.

Chinese proverb

DATE: __/__/__

"YES!"

Today I said "Yes!" to a responsibility:

_____

_____

_____

_____

_____

_____

_____

_____

_____

DATE: _/_/_

"NO!"

Today I said "No!" to a responsibility:

_____

_____

_____

_____

_____

_____

_____

_____

A MAN OF GENIUS MAKES NO MISTAKES. HIS ERRORS ARE VOLITIONAL AND ARE THE PORTALS OF DISCOVERY.

James Joyce

Today's mistake:

_____

_____

_____

Today's discovery:

_____

_____

_____

EVER TRIED.
EVER FAILED.
NO MATTER.
TRY AGAIN.
FAIL AGAIN.
FAIL BETTER.

Samuel Beckett

Today I failed better:

_____

_____

_____

THE GREATEST TEST OF COURAGE ON EARTH IS TO BEAR DEFEAT WITHOUT LOSING HEART.

Robert G. Ingersoll

Today I didn't lose heart:

_____

_____

_____

Never confuse a single defeat with a final defeat.

F. Scott Fitzgerald

Today's single defeat:

_____

_____

_____

DATE: _/_/_

MY HIGH AIM TODAY:

_____

_____

_____

_____

_____

_____

_____

DATE: _/_/_

MY HIGH AIM TODAY:

_____

_____

_____

_____

_____

_____

_____

NOT FAILURE, BUT LOW AIM, IS A CRIME.

James Russell Lowell

DATE: __/__/__

I'm not telling you to make the world better. . . . I'm just telling you to live in it. Not just to endure it, not just to suffer it, not just to pass through it, but to live in it. To look at it. To try to get the picture. To live recklessly. To take chances.

Joan Didion

Today I took a chance:

_____

_____

_____

TO SAY YES, YOU HAVE TO SWEAT AND ROLL UP YOUR SLEEVES AND PLUNGE BOTH HANDS INTO LIFE UP TO THE ELBOWS.

Jean Anouilh

Today I took a plunge into life:

_____

_____

_____

SOMETHING HIDDEN. GO AND FIND IT. GO AND LOOK BEHIND THE RANGES— SOMETHING LOST BEHIND THE RANGES. LOST AND WAITING FOR YOU. GO!

Rudyard Kipling

Range I explored today:

_____

_____

_____

DATE: __/__/__

GREAT THINGS ARE DONE WHEN MEN AND MOUNTAINS MEET.

William Blake

Mountain I met today:

_____

_____

_____

DATE: __/__/__

Dare to be creative in the kitchen today. Cook a:

[ ] PÂTÉ EN CROÛTE

[ ] DUCK PROSCIUTTO

[ ] CASSOULET

[ ] COQ AU VIN

[ ] LOBSTER SOUFFLÉ

[ ] TIMPANI

[ ] SOMETHING SCARIER:

_____

_____

_____

_____

_____

_____

_____

_____

In cooking you've got to have a what-the-hell attitude.

Julia Child

I tried this new recipe today:

_____

_____

_____

What happened?

_____

_____

_____ (What the hell!)

DATE: __/__/__

TODAY I DID MY BEST:

_____

_____

_____

_____

_____

_____

_____

DATE: __/__/__

TODAY I DID MY BEST:

_____

_____

_____

_____

_____

_____

_____

IT IS THE
BOLD MAN WHO
EVERY TIME
DOES BEST,
AT HOME
OR ABROAD.

Homer

WHEN I SEE THREE ORANGES, I JUGGLE; WHEN I SEE TWO TOWERS, I WALK.

▲

Philippe Petit

on why he wanted to cross between the Twin Towers on a tightrope

▼

Today I dared to:

_____

_____

_____

DATE: __/__/__

BECAUSE IT'S THERE.

George Mallory

on why he wanted to climb Mount Everest

Today I dared to:

_____

_____

_____

**GO OUTSIDE
YOUR LINGUISTIC
COMFORT ZONE**

Think about possible languages to
learn and diagram how far they fall
outside of your comfort zone.

terrifying!

reluctant to try

willing to try

my comfort zone

THE ROMANS WOULD NEVER HAVE HAD TIME TO CONQUER THE WORLD IF THEY HAD BEEN OBLIGED TO LEARN LATIN FIRST OF ALL.

Heinrich Heine

Today I ventured outside my comfort zone by saying _____

in _____.

(language)

TRAVELER, THERE ARE NO PATHS; PATHS ARE MADE BY WALKING.

Spanish proverb

New path I made today:

_____

_____

_____

At last he rose and twitch'd his Mantle blue:

Tomorrow to fresh Woods, and Pastures new.

John Milton

Today's new pasture:

_____

_____

_____

DATE: __/__/__

PEOPLE SAID I COULD NOT: _____

_____

_____

_____

_____

_____

_____

_____ (Today I did it!)

DATE: __/__/__

PEOPLE SAID I COULD NOT: _____

_____

_____

_____

_____

_____

_____

_____ (Today I did it!)

THE GREAT
PLEASURE
IN LIFE IS
DOING WHAT
PEOPLE
SAY YOU
CANNOT DO.

Walter Bagehot

DATE: __/__/__

Rate your performance anxiety from 1 to 10.

_____ GIVING A SPEECH

_____ GIVING A TOAST

_____ ACTING ON STAGE

_____ SINGING A SOLO

_____ DANCING IN THE CENTER OF THE CIRCLE

_____ DOING STAND-UP COMEDY

_____ SOMETHING SCARIER:

_____

_____

_____

_____

_____

_____

_____

_____

I'M NOT FUNNY. WHAT I AM IS BRAVE.

Lucille Ball

Today I bravely:

_____

_____

_____

DATE: __/__/__

> *COMMITMENTPHOBIA—*
> THE FEAR OF LONG-TERM
> RELATIONSHIPS OR OBLIGATIONS

Today I:

_____

_____

_____

_____

_____

_____

_____

_____

_____

_____

_____

_____

_____

THE EASIEST KIND OF RELATIONSHIP FOR ME IS WITH 10,000 PEOPLE. THE HARDEST IS WITH ONE.

Joan Baez

Today _____ and I:

_____

_____

_____

OF COURSE I REALIZED THERE WAS A MEASURE OF DANGER. OBVIOUSLY I FACED THE POSSIBILITY OF NOT RETURNING WHEN FIRST I CONSIDERED GOING. ONCE FACED AND SETTLED THERE REALLY WASN'T ANY GOOD REASON TO REFER TO IT.

Amelia Earhart

referring to her flight in the Friendship

My measure of danger today:

_____

_____

_____

AND WHAT HE GREATLY THOUGHT, HE NOBLY DARED.

Homer

Today I thought:

_____

_____

_____

Today I dared:

_____

_____

_____

DATE: __/__/__

TODAY'S DEED:

_____

_____

_____

_____

_____

_____

_____

DATE: __/__/__

TODAY'S DEED:

_____

_____

_____

_____

_____

_____

_____

NOW AT LAST LET ME SEE SOME DEEDS!

Johann Wolfgang von Goethe

"YES!"

Today I said "Yes!" to unsolicited advice:

_____
_____
_____
_____
_____
_____
_____
_____

"NO!"

Today I said "No!" to unsolicited advice:

_____

_____

_____

_____

_____

_____

_____

_____

THE ONLY WAY TO GET RID OF MY FEARS IS TO MAKE FILMS ABOUT THEM.

Alfred Hitchcock

Title of my scary movie:

_____

_____

_____

DATE: _/_/_

Every time I start a
picture ... I feel the
same fear, the same
self-doubts ... and I
have only one source
on which I can draw,
because it comes from
within me.

Federico Fellini

Today I:

_____

_____

_____

DATE: __/__/__

FOR THE PAST THIRTY-THREE YEARS, I
HAVE LOOKED IN THE MIRROR EVERY
MORNING AND ASKED MYSELF:
"IF TODAY WERE THE LAST DAY OF MY
LIFE, WOULD I WANT TO DO WHAT
I AM ABOUT TO DO TODAY?" AND
WHENEVER THE ANSWER HAS BEEN "NO"
FOR TOO MANY DAYS IN A ROW, I KNOW
I NEED TO CHANGE SOMETHING.

Steve Jobs

Something I changed today:

_____

_____

_____

DATE: __/__/__

YOU ONLY LIVE ONCE—BUT IF YOU WORK IT RIGHT, ONCE IS ENOUGH.

Joe E. Lewis

Today I:

_____

_____

_____

DATE: __/__/__

TODAY I SWAM OUT TO:

_____

_____

_____

_____

_____

_____

_____

DATE: __/__/__

TODAY I SWAM OUT TO:

_____

_____

_____

_____

_____

_____

_____

DON'T WAIT FOR YOUR SHIP TO COME; SWIM OUT TO IT.

Anonymous

DREAM LOFTY DREAMS, AND AS YOU DREAM, SO SHALL YOU BECOME.

James Lane Allen

Today I dreamt:

_____

_____

_____

GOD PITY A ONE-DREAM MAN.

Robert Goddard

Dream 1:

_____

Dream 2:

_____

Dream 3:

_____

I like things to happen; and if they don't happen, I like to make them happen.

Sir Winston Churchill

SOMETHING THAT HAPPENED TODAY:

_____

_____

SOMETHING THAT I MADE HAPPEN TODAY:

_____

_____

THEY SICKEN OF THE CALM, WHO KNEW THE STORM.

Dorothy Parker

Today I:

_____

_____

_____

DATE: __/__/__

THE DIFFICULT WE DO IMMEDIATELY. THE IMPOSSIBLE TAKES A LITTLE LONGER.

▲
U.S. Army Corps of Engineers, World War II motto
▼

Difficult today:

_____

_____

_____ (It took ___ hours.)

Impossible today:

_____

_____

_____ (It took ___ hours.)

PER ARDUA AD ASTRA.
(HARD AND HIGH TO THE STARS.)

Royal Air Force motto

Today's stars:

_____

_____

_____

DATE: __/__/__

WHAT I CHANGED TODAY:

_____

_____

_____

_____

_____

_____

_____

DATE: __/__/__

WHAT I CHANGED TODAY:

_____

_____

_____

_____

_____

_____

_____

Change is what people fear most.

Fyodor Dostoyevsky

DATE: __/__/__

Dare to go somewhere alone today:

[ ] TO A RESTAURANT

[ ] TO A BAR

[ ] TO A PARTY

[ ] TO A MOVIE

[ ] TO A CONCERT

[ ] SOMEPLACE SCARIER:

_____

_____

_____

_____

_____

_____

_____

_____

DATE: __/__/__

THE HAPPIEST OF ALL LIVES IS A BUSY SOLITUDE.

Voltaire

Today I:

_____

_____

_____

DATE: ___/___/___

GO OUTSIDE YOUR SELF-PROMOTION COMFORT ZONE

Think about ways to promote your talents and diagram how far they fall outside of your comfort zone.

terrifying!

reluctant to try

willing to try

my comfort zone

You must stir it
and stump it

And blow your
own trumpet,

Or trust me, you
haven't a chance.

W. S. Gilbert

Today I dared to blow my own trumpet:

_____

_____

_____

THE CHARM OF THE BEST COURAGES IS THAT THEY ARE INVENTIONS, INSPIRATIONS, FLASHES OF GENIUS.

Ralph Waldo Emerson

My best courage today:

_____

_____

_____

GENIUS IS TALENT SET ON FIRE BY COURAGE.

Henry van Dyke

My genius today:

_____

_____

_____

DATE: __/__/__

THE RISK I TOOK TODAY:

_____

_____

_____

THE SWEET FRUIT:

_____

_____

_____

DATE: __/__/__

THE RISK I TOOK TODAY:

_____

_____

_____

THE SWEET FRUIT:

_____

_____

_____

THE GREATER THE RISK, THE SWEETER THE FRUIT.

Pierre Corneille

Moderation is the languor and sloth of the soul, ambition its activity and ardor.

François de La Rochefoucauld

My ambition is:

_____

_____

_____

DATE: __/__/__

THERE'S NOTHING IN THE MIDDLE OF THE ROAD BUT YELLOW STRIPES AND DEAD ARMADILLOS.

Jim Hightower

On the sides of my road today were:

_____

_____

_____

DATE: __/__/__

"YES!"

Today I said "Yes!" to temptation:

_____

_____

_____

_____

_____

_____

_____

_____

"NO!"

Today I said "No!" to temptation:

_____

_____

_____

_____

_____

_____

_____

_____

_____

DATE: __/__/__

KATAGELOPHOBIA—
THE FEAR OF RIDICULE

Today I did something ridiculous:

_____

_____

_____

_____

_____

_____

_____

_____

_____

_____

HE DARES TO BE A FOOL, AND THAT IS THE FIRST STEP IN THE DIRECTION OF WISDOM.

James G. Huneker

How I dared to be a fool:

_____

_____

_____

What I learned:

_____

_____

_____

DATE: __/__/__

TODAY I *DID*:

_____

_____

_____

_____

_____

_____

_____

DATE: __/__/__

TODAY I *DID*:

_____

_____

_____

_____

_____

_____

_____

MIGHT, COULD, WOULD— THEY ARE CONTEMPTIBLE AUXILIARIES.

George Eliot

DATE: __/__/__

THERE IS NOTHING LIKE BECOMING A MOM TO FILL YOU WITH FEAR.

Arianna Huffington

Today I:

[ ] DOG SAT

[ ] BABY SAT

[ ] IMAGINED BECOMING A PARENT

[ ] DISCUSSED BECOMING A PARENT

[ ] DECIDED TO BECOME A PARENT

[ ] BECAME A PARENT

How I felt:

_____

_____

_____

ALL OF US HAVE MOMENTS IN OUR LIVES THAT TEST OUR COURAGE. TAKING CHILDREN INTO A HOUSE WITH A WHITE CARPET IS ONE OF THEM.

Erma Bombeck

Today I:

_____

_____

_____

Change is the law of life. And those who look only to the past or present are certain to miss the future.

John F. Kennedy

Change I made today:

_____

_____

_____

CHANGE IS NOT MADE WITHOUT INCONVENIENCE, EVEN FROM WORSE TO BETTER.

Richard Hooker

Today's change for the better:

_____

_____

_____

DATE: __/__/__

YOU ARE TODAY WHERE YOUR THOUGHTS HAVE BROUGHT YOU; YOU WILL BE TOMORROW WHERE YOUR THOUGHTS TAKE YOU.

James Lane Allen

Today I thought:

_____

_____

_____

DATE: __/__/__

A JOURNEY OF A THOUSAND MILES BEGINS WITH ONE STEP.

Lao Tzu

Step I took today:

_____

_____

_____

DATE: __/__/__

WHAT I MADE TODAY:

_____

_____

_____

_____

_____

_____

_____

DATE: __/__/__

WHAT I MADE TODAY:

_____

_____

_____

_____

_____

_____

_____

THE MAN WHO MAKES NO MISTAKES DOES NOT USUALLY MAKE ANYTHING.

Edward John Phelps

DATE: __/__/__

NO TASK IS A LONG ONE BUT THE TASK ON WHICH ONE DARE NOT START.

Charles Baudelaire

Today I dared to start:

_____

_____

_____

WILL YOU, WON'T YOU, WILL YOU, WON'T YOU, WILL YOU JOIN THE DANCE?

Lewis Carroll

Today I joined the dance:

_____

_____

_____

DATE: __/__/__

Dare to drop off the grid for a day (choose one).

[ ] NO PHONE

[ ] NO E-MAIL

[ ] NO SOCIAL MEDIA

[ ] NO INTERNET

[ ] NO TELEVISION

[ ] NO RADIO

[ ] NO NEWS

[ ] NO CLOCK

[ ] NO: _____

What happened?

_____

_____

_____

EVERYTHING IS DANGEROUS, MY DEAR FELLOW. IF IT WASN'T SO, LIFE WOULDN'T BE WORTH LIVING.

Oscar Wilde

Today I:

_____

_____

_____

I HAVE CROSSED THE RUBICON WITH FLAPPING FLAGS AND BEATING DRUMS. . . . IN THIS ENTERPRISE I WILL EITHER LOSE MY LIFE OR WIN HONOR.

Frederick the Great

The Rubicon I crossed today:

_____

_____

_____

I know I have the body of a weak and feeble woman, but I have the heart and stomach of a king, and a King of England, too.

Queen Elizabeth I

How I was a King today:

_____

_____

_____

DATE: __/__/__

TODAY I TRIED _____ AND FELL.

_____

_____

_____

_____

_____

_____

DATE: __/__/__

TODAY I GOT UP AND:

_____

_____

_____

_____

_____

_____

FALL SEVEN TIMES, STAND UP EIGHT.

Japanese proverb

IF YOU TRAP THE MOMENT
BEFORE IT'S RIPE,

THE TEARS OF REPENTANCE
YOU'LL CERTAINLY WIPE;

BUT IF ONCE YOU LET THE
RIPE MOMENT GO,

YOU CAN NEVER WIPE OFF
THE TEARS OF WOE.

William Blake

Today's ripe moment:

_____

_____

_____

What I did:

_____

_____

_____

GRAB A CHANCE AND YOU WON'T BE SORRY FOR A MIGHT-HAVE-BEEN.

Arthur Ransome

The chance I grabbed today:

_____

_____

_____

GO OUTSIDE YOUR DIY COMFORT ZONE

Think about possible projects to try and diagram how far they fall outside of your comfort zone.

terrifying!

reluctant to try

willing to try

my comfort zone

DATE: __/__/__

There's a way to do it better — find it.

Thomas Alva Edison

Today I ventured outside my DIY comfort zone by making:

_____

_____

_____

DATE: __/__/__

SHOPAPHOBIA—
THE FEAR OF SHOPPING

These are the stores that scare me:

_____

_____

_____

_____

_____

_____

_____

Today I shopped at:

_____

_____

_____

_____

_____

_____

_____

CLOTHES AND COURAGE HAVE MUCH TO DO WITH EACH OTHER.

Sara Jeannette Duncan

Today I bravely wore:

_____

_____

_____

DATE: __/__/__

TODAY'S DREAM:

_____

_____

_____

_____

_____

_____

_____ (why not?)

DATE: __/__/__

TODAY'S DREAM:

_____

_____

_____

_____

_____

_____

_____ (why not?)

YOU SEE THINGS;
AND YOU SAY,
"WHY?" BUT I
DREAM THINGS
THAT NEVER
WERE; AND I SAY,
"WHY NOT?"

George Bernard Shaw

DATE: __/__/__

"YES!"

Today I said "Yes!" to an adversary:

_____

_____

_____

_____

_____

_____

_____

_____

DATE: __/__/__

"NO!"

Today I said "No!" to an adversary:

_____

_____

_____

_____

_____

_____

_____

_____

YOU CAN'T TRY TO DO THINGS; YOU SIMPLY MUST DO THEM.

Ray Bradbury

What I *did* today:

_____

_____

_____

THOSE WHO SAY IT CAN'T BE DONE ARE USUALLY INTERRUPTED BY OTHERS DOING IT.

James Baldwin

What I did:

_____

_____

_____

Whom I interrupted:

_____

_____

_____

DATE: __/__/__

Rate your white-coat anxiety. *(Assign each a rank from 1 to 10.)*

____ **DENTIST**

____ **DERMATOLOGIST**

____ **ORAL SURGEON**

____ **PODIATRIST**

____ **CARDIOLOGIST**

____ **ORTHOPEDIST**

____ **RADIOLOGIST**

____ **GYNECOLOGIST**

____ **ACUPUNCTURIST**

____ **OPHTHALMOLOGIST**

____ **GASTROENTEROLOGIST**

____ **SOMEONE SCARIER:**

_____

_____

_____

ATTENTION TO HEALTH IS LIFE'S GREATEST HINDRANCE.

Plato

Today I:

_____

_____

_____

DATE: __/__/__

SENSATIONS TODAY:

_____

_____

_____

_____

_____

_____

_____

DATE: __/__/__

SENSATIONS TODAY:

_____

_____

_____

_____

_____

_____

_____

O FOR A LIFE OF SENSATIONS RATHER THAN THOUGHTS!

John Keats

THE BATTLE, SIR, IS NOT TO THE STRONG ALONE; IT IS TO THE VIGILANT, THE ACTIVE, THE BRAVE.

Patrick Henry

Battle outside won today:

_____

_____

_____

To fight aloud is
very brave

But gallanter, I know,

Who charge within
the bosom

The Cavalry of Woe.

Emily Dickinson

Battle inside won today:

_____

_____

_____

Live all you can; it's a mistake not to. It doesn't so much matter what you do in particular, so long as you have your life. If you haven't had that what have you had?

Henry James

How I lived today:

_____

_____

_____

I DO NOT WANT TO DIE . . . UNTIL I HAVE FAITHFULLY MADE THE MOST OF MY TALENT AND CULTIVATED THE SEED THAT WAS PLACED IN ME UNTIL THE LAST SMALL TWIG HAS GROWN.

Käthe Kollwitz

What I cultivated today:

_____

_____

_____

DATE: __/__/__

TODAY I KNEW WHAT WAS RIGHT:

_____

_____

_____

_____

_____

[ ] I DID IT.

[ ] I DID NOT DO IT.

DATE: __/__/__

TODAY I KNEW WHAT WAS RIGHT:

_____

_____

_____

_____

[ ] I DID IT.

[ ] I DID NOT DO IT.

TO KNOW WHAT IS RIGHT AND NOT DO IT IS THE WORST COWARDICE.

Confucius

IF YOU ARE NOT FAILING NOW AND AGAIN, IT'S A SIGN YOU'RE PLAYING IT SAFE.

Woody Allen

How I took a chance and failed today:

_____

_____

_____

YOU MUST PUT YOUR HEAD INTO THE LION'S MOUTH IF THE PERFORMANCE IS TO BE A SUCCESS.

Sir Winston Churchill

The "lion's mouth" in my life today:

_____

_____

_____

Why not seize the pleasure at once? How often is happiness destroyed by preparation, foolish preparation!

Jane Austen

Pleasure I seized today:

_____

_____

_____

SEEK AND YOU SHALL FIND. ONLY THAT ESCAPES WHICH NEVER WAS PURSUED.

Sophocles

What I sought today:

_____

_____

_____

What I found:

_____

_____

_____

DATE: __/__/__

Dare to explore the outdoors today:

[ ] YARD

[ ] PARK

[ ] COUNTRYSIDE

[ ] WOODS

[ ] WILDERNESS

[ ] JUNGLE

[ ] SOMEPLACE SCARIER:

_____

_____

_____

_____

_____

_____

_____

_____

IN WISDOM GATHERED OVER TIME I HAVE FOUND THAT EVERY EXPERIENCE IS A FORM OF EXPLORATION.

Ansel Adams

Today I:

_____

_____

_____

DATE: __/__/__

TODAY I STOOD LIKE A ROCK:

_____

_____

_____

_____

_____

_____

_____

DATE: __/__/__

TODAY I STOOD LIKE A ROCK:

_____

_____

_____

_____

_____

_____

_____

IN MATTERS OF STYLE, SWIM WITH THE CURRENT. IN MATTERS OF PRINCIPLE, STAND LIKE A ROCK.

Thomas Jefferson

It is not the prize that can make us happy; it is not even the winning of the prize.... [It is] the struggle, the long hot hour of the honest fight.

Anthony Trollope

My honest fight today:

_____

_____

_____

He that shall live this day, and see old age,

Will yearly on the vigil feast his neighbors,

And say "tomorrow is Saint Crispian":

Then will he strip his sleeve and show his scars.

And say "These wounds I had on Crispin's day."

Old men forget: yet all shall be forgot,

But he'll remember with advantages

What feats he did that day.

William Shakespeare

Feats I did today:

_____

_____

_____

FEAR TO LET FALL A DROP AND YOU SPILL A LOT.

Malay proverb

Today I:

_____

_____

_____

MY MESSAGE TO THE WORLD IS "LET'S SWING, SING, SHOUT, MAKE NOISE! LET'S NOT MIMIC DEATH BEFORE OUR TIME COMES! LET'S BE WET AND NOISY."

Mel Brooks

How I was "wet and noisy" today:

_____

_____

_____

DATE: __/__/__

I BUILT THIS DOOR TODAY:

_____

_____

_____

_____

_____

_____

_____

DATE: __/__/__

I BUILT THIS DOOR TODAY:

_____

_____

_____

_____

_____

_____

_____

If opportunity doesn't knock, build a door.

Milton Berle

GO OUTSIDE
YOUR DINING
COMFORT ZONE

Think about different cuisines to
try and diagram how far they fall
outside of your comfort zone.

terrifying!

reluctant to try

willing to try

my comfort zone

THERE SHOULD BE A BURNISHED TABLET LET INTO THE GROUND ON THE SPOT WHERE SOME COURAGEOUS MAN FIRST ATE STILTON CHEESE, AND SURVIVED.

G. K. Chesterton

Today I ventured outside my dining comfort zone by eating:

_____

_____

_____

INNER SPACE IS THE REAL FRONTIER.

Gloria Steinem

How I looked inward today:

_____

_____

_____

I've always seen myself
as a winner, even as a kid.
If I hadn't, I just might have
gone down the drain a couple
of times. I've got something
inside of me, peasantlike and
stubborn, and I'm in it 'til
the end of the race.

Truman Capote

Race I finished today:

_____

_____

_____

DATE: __/__/__

"YES!"

Today I said "Yes!" to a sign from the universe:

_____

_____

_____

_____

_____

_____

_____

_____

"NO!"

Today I said "No!" to a sign from the universe:

_____

_____

_____

_____

_____

_____

_____

_____

DATE: __/__/__

CHANGE I MADE TODAY:

_____

_____

_____

_____

_____

_____

_____

DATE: __/__/__

CHANGE I MADE TODAY:

_____

_____

_____

_____

_____

_____

_____

NOTHING ENDURES BUT CHANGE.

Heraclitus

DATE: __/__/__

NERVES PROVIDE ME WITH ENERGY. THEY WORK FOR ME. IT'S WHEN I DON'T HAVE THEM, WHEN I FEEL AT EASE, THAT I GET WORRIED.

Mike Nichols

How my nerves worked for me today:

_____

_____

_____

My reaction:

_____

_____

_____

DATE: __/__/__

ANXIETY IS THE SPACE BETWEEN THE "NOW" AND THE "THEN."

Richard Abell

Today I:

_____

_____

_____

DATE: __/__/__

HIPPOPOTOMONSTROSESQUIPEDALIOPHOBIA—
THE FEAR OF LONG WORDS

Longest word I dared to use today:

_____

_____

_____

_____

How I used it:

_____

_____

_____

_____

_____

_____

_____

_____

_____

_____

"I FEAR THOSE BIG WORDS," STEPHEN SAID, "WHICH MAKE US SO UNHAPPY."

James Joyce

Words that scare me to use:

_____

_____

_____

DATE: __/__/__

TO STRIVE,
TO SEEK,
TO FIND,
AND NOT
TO YIELD.

▲
Alfred, Lord Tennyson
▼

What I strived for today:

_____

_____

_____

NOTHING VENTURED, NOTHING GAINED.

English proverb

Ventured today:

_____

_____

_____

Gained today:

_____

_____

_____

DATE: __/__/__

MY DREAM TODAY:

_____

_____

What happened:

_____

_____

_____

_____

DATE: __/__/__

MY DREAM TODAY:

_____

_____

What happened:

_____

_____

_____

_____

NOTHING HAPPENS UNLESS FIRST A DREAM.

Carl Sandberg

You may be disappointed if you fail, but you are doomed if you don't try.

Beverly Sills

Today I tried:

_____

_____

_____

DATE: __/__/__

IF NO ONE EVER TOOK RISKS, MICHELANGELO WOULD HAVE PAINTED THE SISTINE FLOOR.

Neil Simon

My risk today:

_____

_____

_____

DON'T BE AFRAID TO FAIL. BE AFRAID NOT TO TRY.

Michael Jordan

What I tried today:

_____

_____

_____

It's too bad that one has to conceive of sports as being the only arena where risks are, [for] all of life is risk exercise.

William Sloane Coffin, Jr.

Risk I took today:

_____

_____

_____

DATE: __/__/__

Dare to get healthy today:

[ ] MAKE A DOCTOR'S APPOINTMENT FOR A NAGGING _____

[ ] JOIN A HEALTH CLUB

[ ] SIGN UP FOR AN EXERCISE CLASS

[ ] START AN EXERCISE ROUTINE AT HOME

[ ] START A HEALTHY EATING PLAN

[ ] LOSE WEIGHT

[ ] GAIN WEIGHT

[ ] SOMETHING SCARIER:

_____

_____

_____

_____

_____

_____

_____

AFTER DINNER, REST A WHILE, AFTER SUPPER WALK A MILE.

Arabic proverb

Today I:

_____

_____

_____

DATE: __/__/__

MY FOOTPRINTS TODAY:

_____

_____

_____

_____

_____

_____

_____

DATE: __/__/__

MY FOOTPRINTS TODAY:

_____

_____

_____

_____

_____

_____

_____

FOOTPRINTS ON THE SANDS OF TIME ARE NOT MADE BY SITTING DOWN.

Proverb

PROBLEMS ARE ONLY OPPORTUNITIES IN WORK CLOTHES.

Henry J. Kaiser

My problem today:

_____

_____

_____

ONCE MEN ARE CAUGHT UP IN AN EVENT, THEY CEASE TO BE AFRAID. ONLY THE UNKNOWN FRIGHTENS MEN.

Antoine de Saint-Exupéry

Today's big event:

_____

_____

_____

DO NOT FEAR TO PIONEER, TO VENTURE DOWN NEW PATHS OF ENDEAVOR.

Ralph J. Bunche

Today I ventured down a new path:

_____

_____

_____

EVERYONE HAS TALENT. WHAT IS RARE IS THE COURAGE TO FOLLOW THE TALENT TO THE DARK PLACE WHERE IT LEADS.

Erica Jong

Today I followed my talent:

_____

_____

_____

DATE: __/__/__

WHEN I LOOKED UP TODAY:

_____

_____

_____

_____

_____

_____

_____

DATE: __/__/__

WHEN I LOOKED UP TODAY:

_____

_____

_____

_____

_____

_____

_____

LOOK NOT THOU DOWN BUT UP!

Robert Browning

THERE IS NO FEAR IN LOVE, BUT PERFECT LOVE CASTS OUT FEAR.

1 John 4:18

Today I:

_____

_____

_____

I HOLD IT TRUE, WHATE'ER BEFALL;
I FEEL IT, WHEN I SORROW MOST;
'TIS BETTER TO HAVE LOVED AND LOST
THAN NEVER TO HAVE LOVED AT ALL.

Alfred, Lord Tennyson

Today I took a chance on love:

_____

_____

_____

"YES!"

Today I said "Yes!" to a dare:

_____

_____

_____

_____

_____

_____

_____

_____

"NO!"

Today I said "No!" to a dare:

_____

_____

_____

_____

_____

_____

_____

_____

DATE: __/__/__

TODAY I UNDERSTOOD:

_____

_____

_____

_____

_____

_____

_____

DATE: __/__/__

TODAY I UNDERSTOOD:

_____

_____

_____

_____

_____

_____

_____

NOTHING IN LIFE IS TO BE FEARED. IT IS ONLY TO BE UNDERSTOOD.

Marie Curie

DATE: __/__/__

GO OUTSIDE YOUR
CHARITABLE
COMFORT ZONE

Today I ventured outside my charitable comfort zone by:

[ ] GIVING MONEY TO A HOMELESS PERSON

[ ] DONATING TO A CHARITY

[ ] WORKING IN A SOUP KITCHEN

[ ] WORKING AT A SHELTER

[ ] VOLUNTEERING IN A HOSPITAL

[ ] VOLUNTEERING AT A SCHOOL

[ ] SOMETHING SCARIER:

_____

_____

_____

_____

_____

_____

DATE: __/__/__

CROWN EVERY PASSING DAY WITH SOME GOOD ACTION DAILY.

Martin Tupper

My good action today:

_____

_____

_____

The credit belongs to the man who is actually in the arena, whose face is marred by dust and sweat and blood; who strives valiantly; who errs, who comes short again and again, because there is no effort without error and shortcoming; but who does actually strive to do the deeds.

Theodore Roosevelt

My arena today:

_____

_____

_____

DATE: __/__/__

ONLY THOSE WHO DO NOTHING... MAKE NO MISTAKES.

Joseph Conrad

What I did today:

_____

_____

_____

Mistake?

_____

_____

_____

Rate your job anxiety from 1 to 10.

___ **LOOKING FOR A JOB**

___ **KEEPING THE JOB**

___ **MANAGING THE WORK**

___ **WORKING ON A TEAM**

___ **WORKING ALONE**

___ **MANAGING A TEAM**

___ **MANAGING THE BOSS**

___ **OFFICE POLITICS**

___ **OFFICE ROMANCE**

___ **BECOMING BORED**

___ **NOT GETTING A RAISE OR PROMOTION**

___ **SOMETHING SCARIER:**

_____

_____

_____

THE ONLY PLACE WHERE SUCCESS COMES BEFORE WORK IS A DICTIONARY.

Anonymous

Today at work I:

_____

_____

_____

DATE: __/__/__

HOW I SPENT MY LIFE TODAY:

_____

_____

_____

_____

_____

_____

_____

DATE: __/__/__

HOW I SPENT MY LIFE TODAY:

_____

_____

_____

_____

_____

_____

_____

Life is ours to be spent, not to be saved.

D. H. Lawrence

DATE: __/__/__

Dare to change yourself today (check one).

    [ ] WORK

    [ ] GOALS

    [ ] COMPANIONS

    [ ] TREATMENT OF OTHERS

    [ ] TREATMENT OF YOURSELF

Today I:

_____

_____

_____

_____

_____

_____

_____

FIRST SAY TO YOURSELF WHAT YOU WOULD BE; AND THEN DO WHAT YOU HAVE TO DO.

Epictetus

What I would be:

_____

_____

_____

What I have to do:

_____

_____

_____

DATE: __/__/__

CYBERPHOBIA—
THE FEAR OF COMPUTERS
OR WORKING ON COMPUTERS

My computer fears:

[ ] LOSING DATA

[ ] BEING A VICTIM OF HACKERS

[ ] CRASHING

[ ] FORGETTING MY PASSWORD

[ ] RECEIVING SPAM

[ ] TRANSMITTING SPAM

[ ] CATCHING FATAL VIRUSES

[ ] INSTALLING UPGRADES

[ ] SOMETHING SCARIER:

_____

_____

_____

_____

_____

Technology... is a queer thing. It brings you great gifts with one hand, and it stabs you in the back with the other.

C. P. Snow

How technology stabbed me in the back today:

_____

_____

_____

What I dared to do:

_____

_____

_____

DATE: __/__/__

TODAY I:

_____

_____

_____

_____

_____

_____

_____

DATE: __/__/__

TODAY I:

_____

_____

_____

_____

_____

_____

_____

IF NOT NOW, WHEN?

Hillel the Elder

DATE: _/_/_

It's not in the still calm
of life, or in the repose of
a pacific station that great
characters are formed. . . .
Great necessities call
out great virtues.

Abigail Adams

Today's necessities:

_____

_____

_____

My actions:

_____

_____

_____

LIFE'S A BITCH.
YOU'VE GOT
TO GO OUT
AND KICK ASS.

Maya Angelou

How I kicked ass today:

_____

_____

_____

WE CREATE OUR FATE EVERY DAY WE LIVE.

Henry Miller

Today I:

_____

_____

_____

Light tomorrow with today!

Elizabeth Barrett Browning

Next year I:

_____

_____

_____

DATE: __/__/__

A list of things that no longer scare me.

_____

_____

_____

_____

_____

_____

_____

_____

_____

_____

_____

_____

_____

_____

_____

_____

_____

_____

CONCEIVED AND COMPILED
by Dian G. Smith and Robie Rogge

COVER AND INTERIOR DESIGN by Danielle Deschenes

POTTER STYLE

www.crownpublishing.com
www.potterstyle.com

ISBN: 978-0-385-34577-4
Printed in China

4 6 8 9 7 5 3
First Edition